CAR BUYING SECRETS

TABLE OF CONTENTS

INTRODUCTION

Most people don't know how to buy a car in today's market

More often than not, when people walk into a car dealership, one of the first questions they have is; "How much is that Ford Focus?" The salesman rattles off the price on the sticker and the customer states that they only want to pay $10,000. What happened here? Simple, the customer just showed the salesman their cards way too early and by doing so, they pretty much gave away their ability to possibly get a better deal through the negotiation process. The reason is, is they already implanted a number in the salesperson's mind that will control the rest of the sales process to get the deal the sales person wants, leaving the customers best interests behind them. The same is true about trade value and payments. So the question is, how do you reduce the stress of buying a car and make the process a lot easier?

To make your car buying experience a lot easier and to get a much better deal, do the following;

Write a list of things that are most important to you

Tell the salesman what's most important to you in a vehicle. For example, safety features, is performance important?, are you more interested in a loaded or more basic car? These are all things that are important to make sure you are getting the right value.

Stay off Price! If the salesman brings up the topic of price get him off of it and tell him you're not ready to talk price and most importantly keep the montly payment that you feel comfortable paying inn your mind.

Always tell him/her that you want to drive the vehicle. A lot of people try to put the cart before the horse. How will you possibly know if the vehicle works for you if you don't drive it? So slow the salesman down and slow down the process.

Keep this in mind;

Knowing this one concept will help bring your anxiety

about looking for a vehicle down to an even keel.

When you talk about prices up front you are giving away the only cards you hold as a buyer. You give the salesman all the tools he needs to work the deal to his advantage.

So don't show your hand and let him/her bring up the price and or trade values. You'll learn more in details in the later chapter

CHAPTER 1

BUYING A CAR TODAY - "THE GAME CHANGES DAILY"

It seems like at least once a week I see an article written by some "expert" on how to save thousands on that new car you want, the fact of the matter is that many times this is true but the method that works for one dealer just might backfire at another. Do your research before you start making offers, visit the sites listed here and find out what others are paying. Know what the invoice amount is for the car you want then find out the supply among local dealers (remember the rule of supply and demand in school).

If these cars are stacking up at the dealers and you have multiple color choices then you are in a stronger negotiating position than if there is only one and it just arrived at the lot just recently. Where you buy is a factor that I never see discussed in these articles either, dealers located in major metro areas are probably paying a

premium for their location and will less able to discount just like the dealer in a small town that has lower overhead but doesn't have the

high sales volume to afford to take a less profitable deal.

Please remember these dealers are independent business owners just trying to make a profitable business deal. The key to any business transaction is "fairness", can both sides live with the deal. Before you buy any car you should know the invoice, any available incentives and/or dealer cash and read the forums to see what others are paying. Be smart and use technology to save you time.

I think some folks go to the extreme when buying a car with the ultimate goal being the dealer makes nothing, like profit is a bad thing. If that is "your" goal, best of luck to you and you may succeed but it may take some time.

I've always placed a high value on my personal time and factor the time commitment into any buying decision. If I know I can save money without driving forever and can have a pleasurable, fast and professional deal without the "brain damage" that inevitably comes with the "best deal ever", I'll always take the easy one.

Do your homework and never, ever make an emotional purchase.

So once you've decided on the car you want it's time to find one or two dealers who you feel have the reputation, inventory and the need to work with you. Assuming you've already done your homework and have an idea what a fair selling price would be it's time to head to the dealer.

Always have your financing arranged before heading to the dealer that way you can work the deal like a straight cash transaction and eliminate a lot of confusion and confusing numbers.

Tip: If there are two identical cars and one has been in inventory longer you might be able to save an extra few hundred or even a thousand depending on the situation (it doesn't hurt to ask), otherwise always try to buy the newest, freshest car on the lot.

When you have found the car you want be prepared to make a committed offer on the car, in other words the the approach many people use is "give me your best deal and I'll think aboutit" and all this will do is get a what is known in the industry as a "low-ball" and you will not be taken sirious, you will get "go to the other dealer get the best price and I'll match it" in this case you will waste more time, or you will get a number that no other dealer can give you so you can come back this is also a waste of time. I personally love my life and want to enjoy it to the fullest this mean my time is very valuable. this is the reason I am writing this book, to help you with the buying process making it easier and painless. Treat car buying like buying a house, check the comps in your area, make an offer that is under you target price but not ridiculous and be prepared to go through with the deal if accepted.

When it comes to financing, the dealer may have a more attractive rate than what you already have secured so be open to saving more money as long as it is a simple interest loan with fixed rate and no prepayment penalties. I will explain in depht in the next charpters

TIPS ON HOW TO BUY CARS

It is very important to know how to buy a car if you want one. There are certain aspects that you should consider before purchasing a new or used. Besides the model, brand name and other features, consider these how to buy a car tips and drive yourself anywhere you want.

Tip #1 - Determine the Car You Want

The first thing that should be in your mind is the kind of car you want. Whether it is brand new or used, you should know what the best one for you is. Think about how you intend to use it, the size, model, brand and the features, and how you intend to purchase it lease, financed or cash

Tip #2 - The Cost of the Car

The next thing to do is to know the cost that you want to purchase. knowing this you will have a clear vision of your budget and how much you are willing to invest. You can go directly in car selling company in your locality or you can check out the price in the internet. Once you are there or have checked the site, it is better to ask assistance from a car sales agent. In this way, the prices are related to you. In the last chapter I disclose the best sites you can go to save money.

Remember to choose a car that will fit your budget only. In case you are acquiring using loans or installment plans, make sure that interests are reasonable enough.

Tip #3 - Inspect the Car

Another how to buy car tips is to check the car you want to buy. This may apply even if the it's brand new or not. It is best to check any paint cracks, if the odometer is working, brakes are in good condition and other features that needs thorough inspection.

In case you do not know when to buy a car that is damaged, you can ask a person you know about cars. In this way, you are able to buy a car that is in good condition.

Tip #4 - Check the Record

It is also important to check the record history of the car you want to buy in case it is second hand. This is to make sure that everything is legal and there will be no hassles in the future after buying the car. later in this book you will have a resource that will allow you to see the history of the vehicle. things like how many owners it had, if it had any accidents, recalls etc.

Tip #5 - Test Drive the Car

One way to find out if the car is in good condition is to test drive it. Well, it is your right to test a car that you want to purchase since you are the customer. In this way, you will determine if the engine is good or there is a problem. Make sure you test the breaks, any funny noises, if the acceleration is normal or it hesitates to speed up.

Tip #6 - Look for the Best Deals

Looking for ways on when to buy a car is also a must. You don't have to rush and just buy a car that you like. It is also a great idea to look for the best deals in purchasing a car.

There are many car companies that will give discounts on cars in the month of December. It means that it is their year-end car sale so take advantage of it because you will save a lot of money. Also look for holidays, as one of the biggest discounts I have seen was in President's day and Memorial day. this is when most manufacturers give dealership insentives and great programs and lastly end of the months.

These are just some of the ways on how to buy a car tips. These guidelines will definitely help you get a new or used car. Just remember, have a safe drive.

CHAPTER 2

BUYING NEW CARS

No matter what you are looking to buy you typically try to find the best deal out there, and I am guessing that it is pretty much a guarantee that if you knew about a great way to get great deals you would take advantage of it. One of the most difficult place to find a great deal is in the car industry where dealer incentives and cut throat industry practices push the prices up and up without consumer say in the process. However, there is one secret that has been kept tight and that most people think of as simply and urban legend that is to buy new cars at the end of the month.

The first reason why purchasing a vehicle at the end of the month can be so good for your pocket is that dealerships force the dealers to maintain a quota, moreover they incentivize them to make more than their quota. The quota is usually tallied up at the end of the month to determine how well each sales person is doing and therefore they are pushed to sell as many cars as possible as the end of the month comes. Furthermore, in desperation to sell enough cars to keep their jobs or receive extra benefits salesmen will often forgo a large profit on vehicles and will be quick to lower the price as the time for meeting their quota comes around. These incentives go beyond the small sales person and the local dealership, the manufacturer of the vehicles often times also offers some incentive to going over quota and also set aggressive sales goals that the dealerships usually have to truly work hard to meet if they have had a slow month.

The next reason why you can milk the salesmen for a good deal by the end of the month is that in recent years with the increase of information available for free on the internet, people have become better negotiators, and the people selling the cars have to rely more and more on the bonuses that they receive outside of their commission which they have to give up to intelligent consumers.

Finally is the fact that the sales managers, who are

responsible for the number of vehicles that the dealership sells in the month and

keeping track of the vehicles on the lot, have to push to sell more vehicles in order to keep the corporate headquarters happy. So now you have to know how to get a good deal, you should start by finding vehicles that they have multiple of. If there are 3 or 4 of the same vehicle sitting on the lot than you can usually get an excellent deal on one of them because the dealership will be hoping to move them out ASAP. Also, the largest inventory will get you the largest discount so going to a larger dealership that is in trouble can get you a vehicle that is much more affordable than going to a small dealership with specialized cars.

Tips For Buying New Cars - What Should You Really Be Careful Of?

Have you ever bought a new car? If you haven't then you are mostly likely looking for tips for buying new cars to help you make the right purchase and get a great deal. If you have bought a new car before, maybe a bad experience has led you to search for more tips for buying new cars! I think what's missing with all these tips that are available online is knowing what really goes on inside the car dealerships and how, after all the tips in the world about that car, you can still walk off that car lot, having lost money.

Don't be another customer who gets fooled by a clever car salesman. Of course you know that most car salesmen work on a commission basis, right? And, in these currently bad economic times, car sales have been decreasing right? Well just those 2 factors combined results in the car salesman doing everything they can to get you to buy the car through a deal that would give them the best commission.

How does a car salesman find his prey? Well, the customer who comes across as plain ignorant is a perfect target! Through your search on tips for buying new cars, have you learned anything about leasing vs buying, pre -paid service coupons, the best day of the month to buy a car, the nice looking extras like "tires for life" or "life time guarantees", the meaning of "pay off your trade", the tactics used to make a deal, and how the "no hassle pricing system" works? Do you know how to negotiate a price down, what questions not to ask and to ask the dealer? There is so much more to buying a car than meats the eye.

Here are some more obvious tip for buying new car, but what will really help you when you walk onto that car lot is having a Car Dealers PlayBook [http://insidethedealersplaybook.info]. A what? A book written for any car buyer looking to buy a car through a car dealership. It's written by an ex car salesperson just like me who got fed up with the lies, corruption and walking a moral tight rope each time he made a car sale. He knows what goes on inside there. Take an inside look into a car dealership and you will be shocked to find out what you read! Save yourself a bunch of money at the end of the day too. I personally have a consulting firm that helps people avoid the paing of going to the dealership, save people thousands of dollars and their valuable time. I attached my consulting company's contact info at the end of this book

It is tough to get a salesman to give you tips on buying a new car. You can try and try to pry the information out of them, but often they do not want to give you what you are looking for. Therefore, most people go out and buy a car without ever knowing what we are getting themselves into.

One of the biggest purchases most of us will ever make is a new car. Sure, most of us will buy a house or a boat or something else that is big, but a car purchase can be a pretty huge purchase for most of us. Especially if it is a new car. Before buying a new car there are some tips that you should know.

- The first tip you should know when buying a new car is to find out your credit score. You should always go in knowing what your credit score is. This will help you to know what kind of financing you will be able to get. You don't want to end up stuck with a high financing rate. Just because the car salesman says that it's the best rate you can get doesn't mean that it is.

- The second tip you should know when buying a new car is to find out what the value of the car is. Do a little bit of research and find out what the car books for. Often car salesmen will lie to you and try to pack more value into the car than there is. They will try to make as much money off of you as they possibly can.

- The third tip you should know when you are buying a new car is the extra offers they try to suck you into. They offer you things like "tires for life" or "free oil changes for life" to try to sell you a car. For many people this is a selling point. You should find out what these car dealerships have to gain by offering you these "special" deals.

There are a lot of tips that I can offer you on how to get buy a new car without all the trickery. Don't let the car salesman get inside your head. Beat him to the bunch.

Control him and make him do exactly what you want him to do, and get the deal that you deserve. If you just do some research and get tips on buying a new car before you just head right out and make this really big purchase you will be a lot better off.

Spend More Time and Less Money Buying a Car

If you hurry when buying your next car, then you will not get the best price. When it comes to buying a car (especially from a dealer), spending a little extra time can result in big financial savings. Here's three areas you can spend a little more time and reap some serious savings:

Price Research −

Before you even go to the dealership to look at cars, you should carefully research how much you should spend on it. It is not good enough to just try and buy the car for a percentage less than the asking price. Some dealers mark their cars up more than others. You might be visiting a dealer that marks his cars up 20% higher than everyone else just so he can look like a nice guy when he cuts the price 20% for you. Visit websites like Edmundsto research dealer "invoice" price for new cars, and blue book prices for used cars. With a little research you can figure out a good deal. If you are not sure what you want, then it may be a good idea to bring a pocket blue book guide with you when shopping.

Talking to Multiple Dealers –

When shopping, never buy a car at the first dealer you visit. Instead, when negotiating price with a salesman, offer a price so low that they will never agree to it. Don't give way very much on the price, but rather wait for them to give the lowest price they are willing to. Then say you will think about it and try and get the offer in writing. Then, when you go to the next dealer, you can use that written offer to try and negotiate the price. You can actually cause them to compete for your business this way.

Waiting For A Sale –

Lately many dealers have been having sales such as "employee pricing." Many of these sales actually result in good prices. So, try and wait for a good sale if you can. If it is near the end of the year this is especially true. Dealers try to meet year in quotas for special perks from the manufacturers, and at the end of the year they may actually sell cars at cost to try and reach a quota so that they can get paid large dealer incentives.

financing

Financing is defined as a means of obtaining the resources to purchase an item, then paying back the loan in a set time period for a set monthly or weekly fee. In most cases, people turn to financing when buying a house, a boat, or a car, but there are instances when financing may be needed to purchase other necessities

pros of financing a car

• You'll have ownership of your car after you payoff the loan.

• You can drive as many miles as you'd like without

limitations.

• You can customize your vehicle any way you like.

• You can build up trade-in or resale value.

• You have the option of driving your car for years to spread out the cost.

• There is no risk of possible lease-end charges

Buying a used car will cost you less upfront than a new car.

Used cars bought through a manufacturer's certified pre-owned program are subject to inspection, making the manufacturer responsible for certain repairs.

Insurance premiums will be lower than those for a new car.

You are the owner (after paying off the car loan).

cons of financing a car

. You'll have higher monthly payments than a lease

• You'll have unexpected post-warranty repair costs

• You'll be responsible for trading or selling your used car if you want a different one

When selecting the right form of finance for your needs and circumstances it is important to weigh up the pros and cons so that you end up with a suitable finance package and do not pay over the odds.

leasing

The lease a car concept instead of finacing is equivalent to driving a new car for less. here we I will disclose some of the Pros and Cons of leasing. things to consider when planing of leasing.

pros of leasing a car

- Leasing gives customers use of an asset of newer, higher specification than the could otherwise buy outright.

- The cost of the asset is paid by monthly instalments rather than a large upfront investment.

- The cost is spread over a period of time and paid

by fixed monthly instalments that will not increase – even if bank interest rates rise.

- Tax advantages – VAT is payable on the rentals, not the purchase price, while rentals may be offset against taxable profit (special rules apply to cars)

- Claim up to 100% of the VAT on commercial vehicles, and 50% on cars (subject to being VAT registered)

- Flexible repayment structures are available, tailored to match your budget.

cons of leasing a car

- The agreement is secured against the asset: therefore if you don't pay, the asset may be repossessed.

- Non-payment can negatively affect the credit rating of both you and your guarantor or Co-signer.

- The finance company are the legal owners

of the asset, and you will not own it.

- The asset is not protected if you or your company are made bankrupt.

CHAPTER 3

CERTIFIED PRE OWNED CAR

Used vehicles sales fell 10% during 2009 after seven years of constant growth. But vehicles that have come off the lease or are resold to dealers and have been thoroughly inspected before sale are a rising segment in the used cars segment. Pre-owned cars are becoming an increasingly important segment for dealers but also for automakers. here's a secret not known by many people. a Certified Used Vehicle goest thru a 160-Point inspection by a Certified Technician, in this inspection the vehicle must pass the requirements of a Certified Vehicle. Items like tires, breaks, fluids, engine, transmission and many more. this will give your vehicle the warranty in some cases same or even better than a new car.

Peace of mind of driving a safe vehicle; the Certified Technician, the Service manager, the Used car manager and the buyer is required to sign the certification document.

Luxury automobile manufacturers began programs for certified pre-owned cars in the early 1990s when cars coming off the lease were traded for new models. For them such vehicles meant maximizing the revenue from their products through cars that have been sold once and which could create brand loyalty.

Certified pre-owned cars are a new category of used cars that offer the advantages of both new and used vehicles. You can get more for the money you pay, just like with some used cars, but you can also rest assured of the quality of the car as it is guaranteed by its manufacturer or another independent agency.

Such vehicles must be inspected, refurbished until they are in an almost new condition and they get certified by either the auto manufacturer or an independent certifying agency. Usually they come with a factory backed warranty, just like a new car.

Certified pre-owned cars are only sold at authorized dealers and can be five years old or less. Typically, they do not have more than 80,000 miles. Another type is the dealer-certified car. These have not been inspected by other authorities outside the dealership. However, they have a warranty or an extended service contract.

Certified pre-owned car programs include extended manufacturer warranties, title verification, roadside assistance, return exchange policies or dealer compliance. One of the most important features is the certification inspection process. When buying a used vehicle, a comprehensive service history is a must. Since the introduction of computerized ignitions or engine-control modules most repairs cannot be done outside dealerships. And there are so many used automobiles that you should always look for the best value for your money.

The status of certified pre-owned car comes with a higher price tag. Compared to other used cars, such a vehicle is closer to a new vehicle in terms of price. Nevertheless, programs for certified pre-owned cars rely on inventory which is quite high due to the decline in the car market. The incentives manufacturers offer through certified pre-owned car programs represent a huge difference for the consumer.

Some of the best selling cars in this category are Lexus RX, Honda Odyssey, BMW 5-Series and 3-Series, Mercedes-Benz E-Class, Toyota Corolla and Camry, Chevrolet Impala, Honda Civic and Accord.

Toyota Camry has been one of the best-selling cars in the U.S. for several years, and there are plenty of used cars that go into pre-owned certified cars program.

Toyota also has one of the best certified pre-owned cars program on the market, including a 160 point inspection and a comprehensive warranty. Toyota Corolla is a very attractive car for younger buyers.

Luxury car manufacturers tend to back their certified pre-owned car programs with the hope that buyers will also become new-car buyers.

Benefits of Buying Certified Pre Owned Cars

The sale of certified pre owned cars has increased 46 percent since 2000. They are considered a more economical option than buying brand new, but they also carry comprehensive safety and quality guarantees from the manufacturer. Most certified pre owned cars are more recent models, so they tend to have all of the advanced technological and performance features found in new vehicles. On top of this, every single one goes through a rigorous process to ensure the utmost quality before it's cleared for sale by the dealership. When searching for a new ride, certified pre owned cars are the best deal.

1. **Inspection** - A major benefit of buying certified is that they all go through 100-point-plus inspections to check for any damaged or broken parts. Each manufacturer has different inspection standards, but the process typically revolves around three aspects: mechanics, safety, and appearance. They check the tires, frame, suspension, glass, lights, brakes, radiator, hoses, belts, fluids, battery, body condition, and exterior surface. Any potential problems are identified and repaired before distribution.

2. **Warranty** - Every vehicle will come with some kind of warranty. Most certified pre owned cars are going to be in good shape, but this document means that the manufacturer will be legally obligated to repair or pay for certain issues that may arise within a certain timeframe or mileage. Warranties vary by

manufacturer, but most range somewhere between 3 months or 3,000 miles to 2 years or 24,000 miles. There is also special coverage for the batteries in electric or hybrid automobiles. If the vehicle carries a third-party warranty, be cautious. This can be misleading because it does not come from the manufacturer and, therefore, it does not provide comprehensive coverage. This could be the case when buying from dealerships that are not partnered with a specific manufacturer.

3. **Roadside Assistance** - Almost all certified pre owned cars include a roadside assistance program just in case anything does go wrong, even if it's your fault. Again, this is mostly a way for the manufacturer to further assure you that they have your back when you buy from them. Toyota for instance gives you One year of Roadside Asistance.

4. **Vehicle History Report** - Finally, it's always good to

know exactly what you are getting for your money. Most of the reputable establishments will offer customers a vehicle history report. The report should tell you about past ownership, maintenance, title history blemishes, faulty odometer settings, flood damage, accident history, and the car title.

If you are thinking of trading in, then make sure to consider certified pre owned cars above all others. After all, any automobile is a big investment, and you want to drive off the lot knowing that you have purchased a safe, high-performance vehicle. Between the warranties, inspections, and other bonuses, there is a lot to love about buying certified pre owned!

Guide to Buying Certified Pre-Owned Cars

If you haven't considered them, you might be missing out on a really good deal with certified pre-owned cars (CPOs).

What Does CPO Mean?

Certified pre-owned cars undergo an inspection that certifies them to be road-ready. There are two main types: dealer level or an underwriting by the original manufacturer.

Dealers certify vehicles after using an inspection checklist. After the vehicle passes, the dealer offers a short-term warranty, typically 30 to 90 days. This process gives you, the buyer, added reassurance that if something should go wrong with the automobile during that period, the dealer will repair it at no cost.

While these warranties are meant to give you peace of mind, there are also limitations. For starters, with a dealer-backed warranty, you have to take the vehicle back to the place where you originally purchased it for the repairs.

If you choose a manufacturer certified pre-owned car,

you get a program that is backed nationwide. The process is streamlined and has the benefit of being honored by any authorized dealer.

Do They Differ Between Manufacturers?

Every program has different criteria. Some limit based on mileage or how old the vehicle is. There are also groups offer special finance rates or even roadside assistance. Others put a provision for a loaner car when your vehicle is in the shop for a warrantied repair. I recomment always asking for a complementary loaner car even if it is not provided.

Each manufacturer has their own list of requirements for their inspection. You can ask to see the checklist so you can verify what is being checked out.

Who Can Benefit?

Anyone shopping for a new or used car can benefit. If

you want a brand new vehicle, there are instances where you can get more vehicle for your money if you purchase certified pre-owned cars. If you are shopping for a used vehicle, then you get the reassurance that the vehicle has passed and extensive inspection. Yes, CPOs are more expensive than their used counterparts. It is up to you to determine if the tradeoff is worth it.

Why Not Buy an Extended Warranty Instead?

If all you are looking for is some peace of mind, you may be wondering why not just buy an extended warranty... it's cheaper! The problem is some of those companies restrict coverage to the extent that only certain areas, such as the power train, are covered. There may be better coverage from a certification. Again my main goal here is to save you money, in some cases you will never get to use some of the warranties anyways.

When you buy a CPO, the dealer or manufacturer has a proven record of accomplishment for standing behind their work. You also don't have to pay a small deductible or pay for the work upfront and then wait for reimbursement.

Certified pre-owned cars give you some peace of mind while saving money on the cost of a newer vehicle.

buying a used car

Sometimes when you feel the need for a car you may find yourself in a situation where you can't afford a new car and will have to settle for used. When you start looking for used car to call your own here are some things that you should know and be prepared for.

One of the first things to do when looking for a used car is to look at the miles driven. You want one that hasn't been driven around so much that it has reached near the end of its productive life because even though these may be cheap compared to others, they are probably not going to be worth the trouble.

Another thing you need to remember is that you buy used cars "as is". Why is this important? It's important because if you find out later that there is some damage that wasn't visible or apparent at first, you are out of luck and will have to fix it or live with it on your own money. So it pays to look closely and to ask about any previous damage history.

You have to be aware of the going prices of the same or similar models manufactured in the same year. This is easily found in the famous "blue book" and blue book value is the language of used car prices. So you will be in a much better position to negotiate a final price if you are armed with this information before you actually show up in the used car lot.

Another thing to look out for is previous damage that the car in question may have suffered. Nowadays, the internet allows you to check the history of the car. Maybe you don't think this is important, but when it doesn't work and you find out that it was in a serious accident, you will be glad that you checked out the history. Today there are Apps that allows you to check some of the vehicle's history, I recommend CARFAX. Some people sell used cars that were actually stolen. You can never be too careful.

The basic thing that you want to accomplish is to make sure that it has been properly maintained. When you know this, you know that there is less likely a chance that it will fail you. There are checklists that you can get to help you to make sure that you go through and check all the things you should check. If you find that you don't know what to check, you should always bring along someone that does.

You would be surprised at what can come off a used car lot so when you take the trouble of preparing yourself ahead of time, you will ensure that you get the best price and the best vehicle in the circumstances.

What to Ask When Buying a Used Car?

Unlike a brand new car, a used car has a history. There is always going to be more uncertainty when buying a used car instead of a new car. Buying a used car can be a much more economical decision since not everybody is in the market for a new car. However, it's important to take the right steps and ask the right questions when considering a used car. You don't want to find out crucial information about the car when it's too late. Before purchasing a used car, ask these questions:

Why Is It Being Sold?

If you are looking to buy a used car from a private seller, find out why it is being sold in the first place. If the seller just bought a new car or the car wasn't even theirs to begin with and they are selling it on behalf of a relative, they may just want the cash and not want to deal with the hassle anymore. This means that they will probably be more willing to negotiate.

What Is the Car History?

Have you heard the term "SHOW ME THE CARFAX"? It's important to know the history of the vehicle and have access to service records. Information like how many previous owners it had and if it was in any accidents should be provided. If purchasing from a dealer, find out if it was a trade in, a lease end taken or if it was bought at auction.

Will Cash Get a Lower Price?

If you are able to pay for a used vehicle with cash, you

may be able to get a lower price. Cash means that the dealer will get the payment immediately in full, so they may be willing to shave some money off of the price tag. Even if cash is not king anymore in this industry never hurts to ask. I say this because dealerships get incentive money from the financing companies when they get you to finance so cash is not as good for them.

Has Any Work Been Done Recently?

In order to increase the value, a dealer may do some work on a used vehicle after they acquire it. This knowledge will help you better establish a fair value of the car.

Are Trade-Ins Accepted?

If you are buying a car, it's likely that you are replacing another car. If you don't want to try and sell the old car on your own, ask the dealer if they accept trade-ins and find out what the offer would be. later on the negotiation section I will teach you how to get more for your trade.

Is There a Warranty?

We know that a certified pre-owned vehicle comes with a manufacturer's warranty. But in a regular used vehicle be sure to understand the terms of the warranty such as how much time or mileage is left on it, before agreeing to purchase the vehicle.

Safety Tips When Buying a Used Car

If you want to make sure you get the best deal when buying a used car, you need to do your research far enough in advance so that you know what you are looking for. In the first place you should obtain a car loan preapproval so you know what your finance limits are. Next, you need to know some of the history of the model vehicle you are looking to purchase.

There are plenty of websites that will tell you about any issues relating to particular models of all manufacturers and it is well worth your while spending some time going through these.

But when it comes to safety issues there are several points you should cover. Let's go over some of them now so you can be sure you are buying a car that ticks all your boxes.

All modern cars in America are fitted with anti-lock brakes and airbags at the very least. Seat belts, of course, are also compulsory additions to all vehicles. Any used-car should also satisfy these requirements but you should ensure that they are in full operational capacity and that the vehicle has passed a safety inspection standards recommended in your state.

We have all seen movies with crash test dummies and most vehicle manufacturers have published the results of these tests. Spend some time online and check out the crash data to make sure the safety standard of the vehicle you are considering meets your requirements.

Always use a qualified mechanic to check your potential vehicle before you start negotiating a price. The inspection should cover the following points.

Seat belts.

Radiator.

Engine.

Lights.

Wipers.

Gauges.

Rust.

Suspension.

Tyres.

Transmission.

Upholstery.

Exhaust System.

Oil leaks.

Accessories.

A road test is also a vital importance and if you can take your mechanic with you it is a good time could e to discuss any unusual characteristics you notice and to pick up any unusual noises. My consulting firm will send you a professional to help you check all these points.

If at all possible buy a car from a registered used-car dealer as this will afford you legislative protection in the event of any future problems. You will also enjoy a limited warranty on the vehicle which can give you added peace of mind.

If you are purchasing the car privately you might want to draw up a contract that gives you a three-month warranty against any mechanical or engine failure.

These used-car buying tips will ensure that you do not end up with a car that fails to meet your predetermined standards. Let's face it, you don't want to end up buying someone else's problemand following the above points will ensure that this does not happen.

Having preapproved car finance is an important negotiating tool which you can use to your advantage. Being able to negotiate a cash price could be the final step which places you ahead of the field.

CHAPTER 4

CARFAX AND REASON WHY TO USE IT

Could it be a mistake to make a vehicle purchase decision based on a CARFAX(TM) report? Are CARFAX(TM) reports always right? Where does CARFAX(TM) get their data? How can CARFAX(TM) know EVERYTHING?

Good questions that millions of people don't ask. They have been hypnotized by an advertising campaign that even the car dealers have succumbed to... dealers who have been in the business decades longer than CARFAX(TM)... dealers who have people on the payroll who can spot paintwork, high water marks, misaligned panels, etc. in a two minute walk-around and ROUTINELY find evidence of negative events that CARFAX(TM) knows absolutely nothing about. But millions of people stop asking questions the moment they read a CARFAX(TM) report that says

'A-OK'... and just as unfortunately, millions more stop asking questions when CARFAX(TM) reports a 'problem'.

There are thousands of auto body repair shops in this country. Their job is to fix cars that have been in accidents and declared repairable by insurance companies. For all practical purposes, if everybody does their job according to industry standards, the vehicles look and drive just like they did before the accident, and continue to provide great service for a normal vehicle life expectancy. For the person who had the accident, this is great... until they try to sell or trade the vehicle.

Once a vehicle gets hung with a 'bad CARFAX(TM) report', it's like YOU having a criminal record, or a REPO on your credit report. Even though you may have paid your debt to society, paid your debt, been wrongly convicted, or had your identity stolen... you are still branded. (That's a favorite term on a CARFAX(TM) report: BRANDED TITLE. It means that the state of registration actually has something on record that they have permanently attached to the title of this car, such as 'salvage rebuild' or 'stolen recovered'.)

CARFAX(TM) is a database. A well organized, cleverly packaged, and marvelously marketed database. CARFAX(TM) has done for vehicle history reports what Xerox did for copiers and Kodak did for cameras and Ipod did for MP3 players. Through their success, their brand becomes the synonym for the product for a period of time.

They get their data from motor vehicle registration records, insurance companies, law enforcement agencies, inspection stations, and auto repair facilities. MOST OF THE TIME, the information is technically accurate, and somewhat useful. BUT, and we have seen this happen on multiple occasions, computer keyboard data entry is SUBJECT TO MISTAKES... and the instant an employee of one of these organizations types in the wrong mileage, the wrong VIN number, etc. and CARFAX(TM) gobbles up the mistake (garbage in...), that vehicle may suddenly have a CARFAX(TM) report with a yellow triangle and a big warning: MILEAGE DISCREPENCY: POSSIBLE ODOMETER ROLLBACK! (...garbage out)

And then, of course, there's that 'fender bender'. The teenage driver comes home with the family car and the right front quarter is smashed. Trees don't call the police and concrete walls don't report to CARFAX(TM). Their insurance rates are ALREADY high enough, so they get this one fixed out of pocket. Very likely, there will be NO CARFAX(TM) ENTRY on this repair, even though it could be THOUSANDS of dollars worse than MILLIONS of other accidents that DID become 'accidents of record' with CARFAX(TM).

SO, is it ever a good idea to buy a car that has a 'BAD CARFAX(TM) REPORT'? It just might be the bargain of a lifetime! One thing is for sure: the dealer that is selling the car KNOWS he has a problem and he wants it to go away. Is his problem the CAR? No... it's the report. The dealer has inspected the car and has no problem with the fact that a body panel has been repainted. He would have no problem pointing this out to a customer who is considering buying the car... a customer who very likely wouldn't notice it EVER because it takes special training to spot good quality auto repair work.

The problem is the REPORT, and the fact that THE REPORT (not the accident and the repair) hurts the value of the car. YOUR job? Get your OWN 'car facts'. If you can see the car in person, ask the dealer to have their most experienced body technician point out what has been done to the car. If you can't see it in person, arrange an inspection BY A BODY SHOP, not by a mechanic. Be sure they put the car on a 'frame machine' and give you a printout that shows how the frame compares to 'factory specs'.

And once you have YOUR data, MAKE A KILLER DEAL and DRIVE A BARGAIN! Need more evidence? What would you think if you found out that one of the biggest and longest term supports of the CARFAX(TM) brand has decided to DUMP them in favor of a competitor? Here's a quote from an official communiqué:

"eBay has entered into an arrangement with Autocheck to provide history reports for every vehicle listed on eBay Motors. The "History Reports" tab will show the full report while there will be a summary just under the bidding section, above the description

Is Using CARFAX a Good Idea?

I recently had the experience of searching for a car with my daughter when her 1996 Lumina bit the dust, literally. She had brought the car in a pinch last year when she needed one fast and it has served her well. But now, a 13 year old car with way over one hundred thousand miles on it, it had given all it had to give.

We started looking for a new car and we learned several things: One, is to do your home work. Always. We researched the cars on the Internet thoroughly, we checked the ratings of each vehicle we were interested in.

We felt reasonably equipped to go out to face the dealers, and were tremendously surprised to find out we weren't. We had picked out the cars we wanted, but they (the dealers) had a different agenda.

We learned some things though. One of the things we learned about was CARFAX. Car Max gave us a free copy for each car we looked at. But researching online we had found some things about CARFAX.

A gentleman in another state had apparently accidentally purchased a stolen car even though he requested a CARFAX report on the car, CARFAX reported the title clean, when actually the car had been stolen. The Title of the car was branded restored and it reduced the value of the car 3 to 5000 dollars.

Another gentlemen ran a routine CARFAX on his car and an accident he knew he had reported was not listed on The CARFAX report.

There were more instances, I am only reporting on two, but does this mean that you should not use a CARFAX report? That they are unreliable?

No, it does not. I recommend using CARFAX, and this is the reason why.

There are many reasons why an accident may not be listed on a CARFAX report. Suppose the person who has the accident cannot afford a regular mechanic and has the car repaired by his best friend Joe down the road? Joe is not required to report the repair he did in his garage so the information is not reported to the DMV or the insurance companies that CARFAX gets their information from.

A stolen car is reported to the police, but the police fail to report it to the DMV, only police department from certain states report to CARFAX.

So it is true sometimes information is missing from

your CARFAX report. But when you are ready to purchase a car one of the ways to get further information is from CARFAX.

CARFAX can and will give you as complete a history as it has at its disposal. Knowing the basic history of the car will help in your decision, but it doesn't take place of a physical inspection. This is always important in choosing a used vehicle.

Are you concerned the car may be stolen? If you are for whatever reason, just take the VIN (Vehicle Identification Number) which can be found in several places on the car. The most convenient is the inside of the windshield on the drivers side, but it is also on the inside door panel, on the engine and on the registration or paperwork of the car.

If you are concerned about the year or the upkeep of the car? This to can be found on the inside of the drivers side door panel. This date is the year of manufacture not the model year which will be one year later. ie a car made in 2005 will be sold as a 2006.

Dealers have their own agenda as I explained on a post on my blog 10 tips on buying a car

As far as CARFAX is concerned, for 40 dollars you can get unlimited reports on as many cars as you like. This is an inexpensive deal when you are shopping for a car. A car is a major purchase, and as in most major purchases a little advance research, and money spent before the purchase will make for better sleeping after the purchase.

10 Reasons To Get A CarFax Report

A CarFax report is affordable. For less than $50.00, consumers can learn everything that they need to know about a vehicle before agreeing to make a purchase and signing on the dotted line.

With a CarFax report, you will be able to confirm the automobile's VIN number, year, make and model. This is important in making sure that you are purchasing the automobile as it is being presented to you for sale.

With a CarFax report, you can find out if the automobile has ever been flooded or has been repaired for any flood damage. This is very important, especially if purchased in areas that are prone to flooding, hurricane damage, etc. Even if an area is not prone to flood damage, there is always the possibility that an automobile has traveled through high water or been exposed to it at some point.

With a CarFax report, you can find out if the automobile has ever been involved in any type of car accident and, if so, what damages were reported. Every day, automobile accidents occur and the damages often require extensive repairs. It is important for you to know whether or not the automobile you are considering purchasing has ever had any type of damage.

With a CarFax report, you can find out if the automobile has ever suffered from any type of fire damage and, if so, what repairs were made to correct the damages.

With a CarFax report, you can make sure the automobile has a clear title and does not have any liens. This is very important when you purchase an automobile, home or even raw land. If you purchase something that does not have a clear title, you are basically throwing your money away. If you receive a clear title, you will have full ownership of the car and will be able to legally resell it in the future.

A CarFax report will confirm the number of miles to be the original miles as noted on the CarFax report. The sad, but honest, truth is that there are some individuals who attempt to falsify an automobile's actual miles in order to collect a higher sale price.

With a CarFax report, an individual can learn how many previous owners the car has had. This is important in considering why the car has had multiple owners, if it has, and may be a sign that something is wrong. An automobile with only one owner is more likely to be reliable as opposed to one that has been shuffled amongst multiple owners.

With a CarFax report, you can find out what, if any, repairs have been made on the automobile. This is important in considering what type of recurring problem there may be with the automobile or whether or not you are purchasing a lemon. A car that has had excessive repairs, either in various parts or in one particular area, may be an indication that you should be prepared to spend some time at the repair shop as the new owner.

And finally, a CarFax report provides overall peace of mind in knowing that you did the research and are not relying on the seller to provide accurate information. An informed buyer is a smart one. For more visit this link on (www.carfax.com).

Chapter 5

SALES NEGOTIATION PRACTICE - HOW TO BUY A CAR

So let's spend some time talking about something that we can all relate to: buying a car. It's all good and fine to talk about negotiating concepts, but buying a car is when the (pardon the pun) rubber really hits the road. Nobody that I know ever looks forward to the whole process of buying a car. here we will learn some of the valuable words and what to say when buying a car. remember you buy a car every three, four or more years but a salesperson sell cars for a living so they will know all the objections a regular customer has. In this section I will prepare you to negotiate like a champ and beat the salesperson.

Although you want a car, you don't want the hassle that you have to go through to get one. For the purposes of this discussion, we

won't care if you are looking for a new or a used car -

the process is basically the same. Let's see if we can make things just a bit easier for you the next time you need to go car shopping.

Keep in mind I teach these same negotiation process to all my students and my consultants. When I go with buyers to the dealership I use these concepts over and over again. I have saved thousands of dollars to so many people and will aslo help you keep some money in your pocket.

Determine Your Schedule:

This will set the tone for the whole car buying process: how much time do you have before you need to have a car? The more time that you have before you need to make a decision, the more power you have. If you currently have a car to drive or if you walk/bike/run everywhere and can keep doing so, then you are (another pun) in the driver's seat. You can take your time in selecting the brand, model, and sales location that you want to buy from. If things aren't going your way at any time, you can just stop the process and

restart it whenever it suits you. On the other hand, if your clunker just gave up the ghost and you really need a new set of wheels, like yesterday, then you have less negotiating power, but you can maximize what power you do have. You do this by spending more time on the car search right now and doing your research thoroughly and moving quickly. If you spend more time now, then you'll have all of the information that you need and you can lead the negotiations.

Find Out What You Want:

Negotiations can't start until you decide exactly what you want. If you already know, then great move on to the next step. If you don't know, then this is the time to do some off-line research and then go do some test driving. No matter what the "helpful" salesperson says, keep in mind that you are not a car buyer right now - you are a car shopper and so your one and only job is to decide what make and model you want. Don't sweat options and maintenance packages right now - just pick a car!

Research How Much This Car Should Cost:

Ah, isn't living in the 21st Century great? Thanks to the power of the Internet you can go online and quickly find out how much your dealer paid for. A great place to start is Edmunds.com and Trucar.com. If you need to understand the difference between Manufacturer's Suggested Retail Price, Dealer Invoice price, etc., then checkout an excellent overview at WikiAnswers. Once you know what a reasonable price is, then you are ready to negotiate.

Remember that the goal of the dealer is to make the

most money and your goal is to save the most money.

Negotiate the Price.

So the first thing you need to do is to call every single dealer in your area to find out what is the lowest price they are willing to take for a specif car that you are looking for. If they want to earn your business they will give you their real numbers over the phone so you both don't have to waste time. If they tell you that you need to go to the dealership in order to give you the real numbers then don't even botter doing business with them. because chances are that they are not full disclosure anyways. in this phone call your main goal is to lock in the price of the car. some dealerships will have their BDC department that takes the incoming phone calls and they are supposed to give you all the information you need to know.

For this process we are going to use an example you

you buying a used car advertised at $15,995. and we are going to negotiate it the most we can.

One of my mentors thought me this one powerful question that saved me thousands of dollars up until today and now I pass it on to you. "What's the least you can take for it and be ok?" at this point the salesperson will tell you straight up the lowest they are willing to take for the car or lie to you. You will find out the truth keep reading

Own The Stage:

When you go to a car dealer to start negotiating, it is as though you are walking onto a stage. This is one of the reasons that so many people fear buying a car - they've got stage fright. Ideally you want the salesperson to be eager to talk to you so you should do you best to set things up in your favor. We all know that car dealers want to move as much inventory as possible before the end of the month/year. If you can wait until that time is drawing close, then you'll improve your position. No matter what, make sure that you have all the time in the world to talk to the car dealer because that

will put you in control of the discussion. The salesperson won't have the same amount of time and so you'll be in control. So we are going to ask for $14,500. why not more? here's why with the power of the internet today all dealerships are in competition to earn your business and they will post their lowest price online to bring you to the dealership. So the advertised price has little room to negotiate, in some cases the dealer will tell you that they can't go any lower.

The Last Word Said Is The Most Important

Realize that even after you've reached a fair price for

your car, the salesperson is still participating in the negotiating game - it's not over yet. You need to stay awake and engaged because this is where the money can slip out of your wallet / purse. Taxes, documentation, dealer prep are all negotiable items and the salesperson is going to want to present them to you as fixed items to bring the already low price they have advertised. Don't give up now!

The one thing you need to focus on is the actual price of the car, if the salesperson is not walking you out of the dealer because your offer is too low and they are not making any money then you still have some room to negotiate.

So at this point the salesperson will go to his manager with your offer and come back saying the lowest we can do in this car is $15,500. at this point you don't know if this is true or not. so you will ask again for your original $14,500 or let them know you will leave the dealership. at this point the salesperson will go back to the manager with your offer. the salesperson will come back with a counter offer of $15,200 and will say this is the absolute best price they are willing to do. keep up with me know, say the following " I saw another car at the other dealership with about the same miles for lower so if I don't get this price I will be going over there". So the salesperson will go back to his manager again with your offer. At this time the manager will come to you with the salesperson to tell you the real absolute lowest they are willing to do for the car of $15,000. between you and me at this point you know they are telling you the truth I told you the reason why before (the power of the internet). So take the deal and shake their hand. One point to keep in mind be respectful at all time ot the negotiation process, all we are looking for is a fair price anyways. here I am not teaching you to low ball or sound cheap because you will be asked to leave the dealership and miss out on a deal. So keep professional at all times and smile often. Be likable, I have seen so many people thrown out of the dealership because of their arrogance. So keep calm and earn your respect. the same way I saw so many very good deals happen for people who were charismatic and the sales manager liked them.

One quick note: If the negotiation is not going in you favor, use this powerful letal words that make the salesperson and even the managers afraid. ***"I'll think about it"*** this sentence along have saved thousands of dollars to many of my customers. One thing to know is that the dealer is about to lose a customer and will make everything possible to keep you as a customer. this mean lowering their price or saving you more in your monthly payments.

Avoid Dealer Fees:

There are some Dealer fees that you can avoid, like dealer prep fee, documentation, destination etc. keep aware of some fees and if you ask nicely they will remove them or give you a break. when I take my customers to the dealership I know exactly what to pay and what to avoid, again my intention is to save you the most money. if you have a trade pay attention to the next section.

No matter what information I can pass on to you, buying a car will always be an experience that causes emotions to run high simply due to the amount of money that is involved. If you follow these simple steps, you can at least be more calm and focus on achieving the outcome that will make you a happy driver for years to come.

TRADE VALUE

In this section we are going to learn the ways you can negotiate your trade. the main purpose of this is to get the most money for your trade. in some cases you will go almost to the same process as if you are negotiating the car you are buying. I will give you the straight no BS process to follow. for this you will also do your research on the value of your car. you need to go online to sites like KBB.com and see the around value of your car so you don't go with high expectations and be disappointed. Once you do your research set your mind what is the least you can take for your trade and be ok. keep this number in your head.

First: In order to get more for your trade you have to be conscious of how your car looks. Obviously this includes how clean it looks, does it have damages, scratches, dents, need tires etc. but for this we are going to put a "MAKE UP TO THE TRADE". This mean make it as nice as possible with the less amount we can spend.

Second: Once at the dealership the Used car manager will inspect your trade. to see what numbers they will give you. Remember in this case they are looking to give your the lowest possible and you are looking to get the highest possible. So for example they will give you a number and say "the book value on your car is $1,500" you will act surprised and san "NO" ask for more like $3,300. The salesperson will go back to his manager with your offer. after few times of back and forth if the numbers are close to your number in your head just take it and shake their hand.

Sometimes it makes more sense or you will get more money if you sell it privately. and it's perfectly ok to say no to their offer and sell it on your own. To my customers in my consulting firm I will tell them if the dealer is not giving you what you need just take the trade out of the deal and sell it out. maybe a family member or a friend who needs a car. they will appreciate you and thank you more believe me.

Remember. We are looking for a fair number we are not looking to be a low baller or ask ridiculous number for a trade.- ask this powerful question; What's the most you can give me and be ok for my car?

Should You Insure Your Car at Market Or Trade Value?

Many people ask whether they should insure their vehicles at market value or trade value. There is no correct answer; it all depends on the car and your personal circumstances. Let's first define these terms, often used incorrectly. Retail value is the price you paid for the car, e.g., 100,000 currency units.

Trade value is the price you would receive (reasonably) if you traded the vehicle in for another, e.g., 20,000 currency units if you're a rough driver and the car was actually inherited from your grandmother. Essentially this is the price a trade-in establishment would give you, taking their profit into consideration. Replacement value is what you would pay to buy a similar car today. It covers trade value but also takes into consideration private sale.

Market value is the average of retail and replacement value, i.e., 60,000 currency units. It is the amount you could reasonably have sold it for before it was stolen/ damaged/ you decided to sell it. (Reasonable means fair and average, not the price you're 'trying to get away with'.)

You can decide whether you want to insure your car at its market value or its replacement value. The latter will cost you a little more; more importantly, insurance companies often stipulate they will replace your car only in the first year or two. After that, as you can understand, it becomes too expensive for them. You should revalue your car each year. When you insure a vehicle, you must keep adjusting your premium in accordance with its changing value. If you start out with a new Mercedes Benz and pay an exorbitant premium for this top of the range car for a number of years, you may find down the line that the market value of second hand Mercs has dropped dramatically and it would have been worth your while rather to bank those hefty premiums over the years.

On the other hand, if you inherited a Rolls Royce from your granddad and it's still running, it may soon be worth a lot more than the petrol it runs on (probably quite a lot) and worth insuring well. A car loses value all the time, from the time you trade your old vehicle and have to pay the middle man who takes your car, to the time you drive it out off the showroom floor and start adding mileage to the clock, to the time wear and tear starts to take effect; not to mention the changing market, including the price of new cars and fashion or demand for certain types of vehicles. In summary, trade value is a sensible way to value your car, bearing in mind that you kind of know that you're losing a set amount for the convenience of someone else doing all the hard work. But market value, if you've looked after your car, could be a more realistic indication of what the car is worth to potential buyers. All you need to do is research similar makes and models in local newspapers. Replacement value is the most expensive option and unless you are adamant you want another vehicle just like this baby, you're likely to pay more in insurance premiums than the car is ultimately worth. But do choose one of these options. According to the South African Insurance Association (SAIA), around 65% of the cars on our roads today are not insured. It's bad enough not being insured, imagine being involved in a prang with another motorist who is also not insured! There is another option for ensuring your car is insured at its real value. It's called top-up-insurance and is usually taken up when a vehicle is purchased through finance. How does it work? If you buy your car on finance, the insurance policy is ceded to the company through which you receive your loan. If for some reason you need to make a claim, the insurer will first pay the finance company to settle the outstanding finance debt, which leaves you debt free (to a certain extent). Another policy you may be interested in investigating, particularly if you purchase a pre-owned vehicle, is mechanical warranty insurance. This policy would however only be of value to you if you're running a up market car. If you're driving a runabout, a good service every 10,000kms will be decidedly more cost-efficient. For more visit this link on (kbb.com).

CHAPTER 6

GAP INSURANCE AND OTHER WARRANTIES

So you're just about to buy your next new car. You have the deal you want, the part exchange value seems palatable, and you can't wait to get your new car. Sound familiar?

Thousands of motorists choose to buy their cars from main franchised dealerships each year. This is mainly due to the fact that they have a wide choice of vehicles, often sold as part of the manufacturers used car scheme, they also provide warranties, a mechanical check, and an element of peace of mind for the consumer.

If you are buying a new car you will almost certainly have to visit a franchised dealer as most of the Internet based sellers are merely brokers acting as middle men between the consumer and franchised dealer.

Selling you a car is not the only thing the dealer has in mind!

Due to the current economic climate we live in, and the ever growing ease at which you can obtain information over the Internet, many dealers can no longer survive by selling cars alone.

Most car dealer groups have dedicated finance departments specifically designed to sell finance and insurance products such as gap insurance, extended warranties, tyre insurance and other insurance related products. Main dealers and car supermarkets now budget to make as much money from finance and insurance as they do from the actual car sale. Most car dealers will aim to make around $800 profit on every car they sell, whether new or used, with almost 50% of that profit coming from finance and insurance products.

The growth in popularity of these types of insurance products has resulted in dealers targeting their sales teams to sell gap cover on every car they sell. However, policy costs can vary dramatically when purchased from a car dealer or car supermarket.

So how much should you pay for a gap insurance policy?

Recently we carried out a survey of main dealers, car supermarkets, and a number of independent dealers and found a startling array of gap insurance prices.

The average cost of a gap insurance policy at main franchised dealers is around $399 for a policy that will cover vehicle replacement up to the value of $15,000.

Prestige car franchises such as BMW, Audi, Porsche and Mercedes appear to be exploiting the popularity of this type of insurance even further with prices as high as $1000 for a vehicle replacement policy. Most prestige franchised dealers calculate gap insurance prices based on a percentage of the vehicle selling price resulting in sky high policy costs!

Many dealers now employ Business Managers specifically targeted to sell finance and insurance. So don't be surprised when you get the heavy sell! The dealer will want you to buy a gap policy and so will the sales person!

Buying on the Internet!

Like most things sold on the internet nowadays, you can save a lot of money when purchasing gap insurance from the growing number of online gap insurance providers. Cost savings from not having to pay rent on fancy showrooms combined with high commissions paid to the sales team's means that the cost of buying a gap insurance policy online can be as much as 75% cheaper than a franchised dealer.

Setting up a gap insurance policy online is also very simple and can be completed in a matter of minutes by completing a short online application form. You can also speak to someone over the telephone if you have any questions or queries.

In addition to the cost saving, most of the online gap insurance providers make it very easy for you to select the correct policy for your needs with clear and concise product descriptions and key benefits as well as the obligatory T&C's and policy details, which can all be downloaded.

I also tell my customers to ask if their insurance carrier provide Gap Insurance if so It will be cheaper than buying it out of the dealership.

Car Warranty For Peace of Mind

However you look at it purchasing a new or used vehicle gives you a lot to consider. Obtaining car insurance and gap insurance, on top of the cost of maintenance can be very expensive. Perhaps this is a reason why it is so easy to overlook the danger of breaking down on the side of the road. A family vacation can be ruined in an instant by an unforeseen breakdown. This is easily avoided by purchasing an extended warranty.

Stop Living in Fear

A car is something that isn't optional for most people. Transportation that's reliable is crucial, more so if you have a job to get to each day, ferrying children around and responsibilities to handle. It often seems like a car's mechanical woes begin as soon as its manufacturer's warranty expires. From there on out, you have to live in fear of breakdowns and other issues. Going through all that is not necessary, with a high rated vehicle service contract that protects you?

Breathe Easy with an Extended Car Warranty

Even if you are conscientious about taking care of your vehicle's routine maintenance, there's no guarantee that it will keep running like a champ. Anticipating what will happen is crucial, even more if you want to live stress free. With a top of the line Car Warranty in toe, you can have a vehicle without the fear of repair bills corrupting your peace. The best part is, that peace of mind can be yours for an incredibly low price. Because most sellers will break the payments into low monthly installments to be paid over a year.

Extended Warranties Make Sense

As much as you rely on it, your vehicle is one thing that you should protect at all costs. Keeping it as long as you can is a very smart move financially - Huge breakdowns will dismantle your schedule. The bottom line is, if you own a vehicle, an extended warranty is a worthwhile investment. The peace of mind that the right car warranty will afford you is absolutely priceless. stop losing sleep about huge repair bills - purchase a car warranty before its to late. be honest with yourself, has any of your vehicle`s not had a failure of some kind. Its when will your car have failure, not will it.

lemon laws and extended warranties – what you should know

Lemon law are regulations enforced by various states that protect customers from defective vehicles. Different states have different rules when it comes to lemon laws, but most of them share some common aspects.

For example, lemon laws require that the problem

with the vehicle be taken care of by the manufacturer, not the car dealership. There are certain characteristics a vehicle must meet to be qualified as a lemon. If a car is worked on repeatedly for the same issue and the issue keeps re-occurring, then the car will most likely be designated a lemon. If you purchase a lemon, you are often entitled to some sort of compensation that deals with how much you paid for the vehicle and how many miles are on it. As stated before, different states have different lemon laws.

Some states cover used cars under their lemon laws, while some only cover new vehicles. There are many websites where you can find out your state's particular policy regarding lemon vehicles. Simply go to the search engine of your choice and type in your state's name followed by 'lemon law.' You will then be presented with multiple websites that can educate you on your particular state's policies regarding lemon laws.

So...even if your state has a lemon law, do you need an extended warranty? The answer is a definite yes. Cars that are not qualified as lemons can suffer wear, tear, and component failure. If your state does have a lemon law, it's still quite prudent to purchase an extended warranty. Problems with a vehicle do not necessarily qualify it as a lemon, and that's a crucial fact you need to understand when considering purchasing a warranty. If you fail to purchase an extended warranty and end up needing repair, it's unlikely that your state's lemon laws will cover you, unless of course the vehicle has experienced the same problem multiple times with no record of satisfactory repair after numerous attempts.

There are many types of extended auto warranties available. You can purchase one from the dealership where you got your vehicle, or go to the source and deal directly with a company that specializes in extended auto warranties.

What your warranty will cover depends on what kind of policy you choose. Ideally, you will want a policy that covers parts and labor, as well as wear, tear and breakdown. Some plans will require you to pay a deductible, others won't.

Be sure to do your research and choose a warranty provider and plan that suits your needs and your budget. By being educated, you can save yourself a lot of trouble and avoid being duped into getting a policy that you do not want. Before shopping for a policy, be clear on what you need, and don't let slick salespeople convince you otherwise.

Car Insurance Policy

There are many things to take into consideration

when attempting to choose the best car insurance policy for your insurance needs. The most important item is the experience of the company from which you are taking car insurance policy. Some insurance companies' policies are nothing more than facades to take your hard earned money.

They have no experience in the car insurance industry and have no intention of ever paying an insurance claim. By choosing a company with experience and, ideally, a large presence in the industry, you will ensure that you are dealing with a reputable company that stands by its claims.

At that time, people with Car insurance policy still had to contact as agent to insure vehicles, however the company began offering online quotes and service for motorcycles, boats and recreational vehicles, the first company to do so. Since then, the response for insurance for these types of vehicles has continued to grow.

Fender-bender about Car Insurance Policy:

Car Insurance Policy is a very important item these days. It is so important that some states have required that every citizen that holds a driver's license has to be insured by a Car Insurance Policies to legally drive on their roads. There are many car insurance company policies in the industry right now that are competing for your business. So how do you know you are choosing the car insurance policy to fit your car insurance policy needs?

Private Damage Security:

This is the component of a car insurance policy that has to do with private damage security from of damage to the policyholder and the inhabitant of the underwrite automobile. For delicate wound shelter you really need to take some time and give your own person position some watchful thought, so that you can judge the in general impact that an misfortune connecting wound could importance in having on you and your dear ones. It may be repugnant, but by doing this you will be able to make sure that you are properly protected.

Conversely, it does not have to be your car insurance policy that provides you with the financial windfall that will divert economic disaster in the face of a liability claim. How can this be? Because if the other driver is at fault and is properly insured, then you will be able to collect money that you would never had been able to collect if the driver was uninsured. Hence, information about car information policy is mandatory.

Tips on How to Find the Right Car Insurance Policy

Who needs car insurance? Anyone who owns a car and wants to drive it on public roads needs car insurance to protect themselves against theft or costs that occur due to automobile accidents.

These days, one is really left pampered for choice when it comes to acquiring car insurance because there are a lot of policies and a wide array of insurance companies to choose from. So wide is this arena that at times it could leave one confused as to which policy to purchase especially when one is a first time buyer of these insurance policies.

First things first, you should consider the details of such insurance when thinking of buying one. These details include your driving history, experience in driving, your age, and the model of your car. The rule of the thumb here is that the younger the policy holder is, the costlier would be the insurance policy because of the driver's inexperience and young age.

However that is not the only factor deciding the cost of your insurance policy, if you happen to have a bad driving history or a bad track record then you will obviously have to shell out much more than the person having better driving record than you. So this means that only experience, safe and reliable drivers get to have car insurances at a comparatively cheaper rate. Sometimes it can also be very hard for a person having a tarnished record and a record of a lot of major accidents.

The most important thing that one should bear in mind while trying to get a car insurance is to never purchase the insurance policy without conducting a comparison of quotes. One should keep in mind that the insurance policies for car does not feature the same rate everywhere and while some companies may offer discounts and good deals, others may not. So in order to make the most out of your car insurance, make sure you don't forget to get quotes from different insurance companies and compare them so that you can pick the best one.

While finding the right insurance company may seem like a daunting task, but if one puts in the effort to search around, research and compare then one can easily make the best investment. It is better to get a good and worthwhile policy the first time around instead of constantly switching from one insurance provider to the other undergoing a lot of unnecessary stress and hassle. So take the time out to find the right company so that you can stick with them for a long period of time.

Differing Categories of Car Insurance Policies

Everyone in the country knows the importance of car insurance policies. In fact, most citizens of the country understand the importance of insurance long before they actually start driving a car by watching their parents. However, when it comes to buying the insurance for the first time in their lives, the whole process takes some getting used to. The reason for this is simply the variety of options available in the market.

If you have just started researching the insurance industry, then you have already come across the differing categories that these policies can be grouped under. The salesperson can also refer you or help you get low insucarnce coverage.

Comprehensive policy:

These are policies that go all the way when it comes to protecting your interests. Apart from each and every policy feature of the policies mentioned above, these policies also cover you against damage to your car from some accident and personal injury. These policies are particularly created to take into account every possible contingency that can arise on the road.

Needless to say, since the coverage provided by these policies is so detailed, they are the most expensive of the lot.

Even though the comprehensive policy is the most expensive, it is also the most useful and beneficial policy in the market. However, if it is only the money factor that is putting you off from buying these policies, then you can sidestep it neatly by simply comparing multiple car insurance quotes from different online providers. Car insurance quotes are like semi formal offers from online providers which take into account all your background and your requirements. By comparing multiple quotes, you can easily find an affordable comprehensive policy from the many policies that are available online.

CHAPTER 7

FASTEST WAY TO INCREASE YOUR CREDIT SCORE

The fastest way to improve your credit score is easier than you may think. Without a doubt the most common failure amongst those that want to improve their finances is not taking action. It can be easy to in a sense try to avoid your problem by trying to not think about them or ignoring any warning signals. A classic symptom of this is to not open your post or mail if you suspect it is a bill or demand for payment. Another classic sign is ignoring phone calls unless you know the identity of the caller.

If you can identify with any of the above symptoms then now is the time to put an end to it and start taking action. All you need to do is to promise yourself to take action every single day. Even if you only spend 15 minutes each day trying to improve your credit score you will be amazed at how much progress you will have made after just one month. You will not only benefit from the tangible positive effect on your credit score, you will also feel so much better about your debts and significantly more empowered for having done something to improve the situation.

By performing small daily tasks to improve your rating you will become so much more aware of why things gt so bad in the first place. You will find yourself becoming more and more aware of your money management and becoming more diligent during your everyday activities. This little and often approach will help prevent you from slipping back into your old habits or careless spending or mismanagement of your finances.

7 Ways to Increase Your Credit Score

There are easy and hard ways to increase your credit

score. There are short term and long term ways to increase your credit score. And, there are straightforward and sneaky ways to increase your credit score. This article will show you seven methods of increasing your credit score.

1. Get Rid of Negative Marks -- Did you know you can challenge any negative mark on your report? If it is a real mistake on the credit bureau's part, they have to remove it under the law. But even if it's legitimate, they often won't go to the trouble to "prove" it and thus, they have to delete it.

2. Pay Your Debts in a Timely Fashion -- This might fall into the "hard,""straightforward," and "long term" strategy categories, but it works.

3. Pay Down Your Revolving Debts -- Revolving debts like credit card bills, should never exceed 30 percent of the maximum allowed amount.

4. Keep a Reasonable Number of Accounts -- Having too many accounts can hurt you. But so can having too few. Ideally, you will have between 3-5 revolving lines of credit.

5. Consolidate Debt -- If you have a high amount of consumer credit and can consolidate it into an installment loan (a.k.a. home equity loan), it will help your score. This was easier a few years ago, but if you can do it these days, it will still help your credit.

6. Avoid Subprime Loans -- You'll pay a premium for these loans in terms of the interest rates. If you can't afford it with a regular loan, you can't afford it.

7. Use Your Consumer Statement -- If you can't get the credit bureau to remove a black mark, you do have the right under federal law to post a 100 word response that all future creditors can see.

Take advantage of all of the options you have to

increase your credit score.

Credit Score Chart

Credit score chart is a report of your recent credit history. It is actually the FICO score with some other related information. According to FICO the credit score could be any number from 300 to 850 depending on the history of your credit. In simple words it is an expression based on the statistical analysis of a person's credit files and it is used to represent the credit worthiness of that person.

Basically credit score charts are used by the financial institutions, banks, and credit card companies to evaluate the risks in case of lending money to consumers and to lessen losses due to bad money owing. Credit scores are also used to decide whether the applicants are capable for loans. If they are qualified, it also helps to determine the interest rates and credit limits they should get.

There are two major facts that we need to know when we are dealing about the credit score chart. Firstly, we need to understand the five main factors that are used to find out the credit score of a person and how these factors are selected. After that we need to know how to read and understand a credit report. These are mentioned here under. Firstly thirty-five percent of the score depends on the record of timely payment of loan. Then thirty percent of score is calculated based on others debts, unpaid bills and total outstanding balance.

Fifteen percent of the rest is dependent on how long you are using the credit system and the history of that time. Ten percent depends on the types of credit and the number of credit account. Ten percent depends on new accounts and types of account recently opened. The score you achieve in FICO credit score chart classifies you in different groups and provides you different types of facilities.

If your credit is between 700 to 850 it would be called an excellent score. For this score you will be eligible for any kind of loan with lowest interest rate. For this reason you will be under fair repayment terms. If the score is between 680 to 699 you will be easily approved for any kind of loan from your lender. Score between 620 and 679 is considered as the reasonable score. The people under this category will be approved for any kind of loan but they will not be able to get the best interest rates. Scores between 550 and 680 will not allow you to have loan of any amount. Some lenders may agree to give you loan but you have to pay it back with highest rate of interest.

The people who have scores under 550 can hardly have any loan as the lenders feel insecure in the case of repayment. They must concern with credit repair before taking any kind of loan. The credit score chart is designed in such way that one can easily have an idea of one's recent financial condition in case of loan, debt bill payment etc. Find out more about under credit score click this link www.emgtoday.com/fix.

Here's a little gift from me to you, if you are under collections of looking to make a payment arrangement with a creditor use this simple form and send it to all your creditors. believe me a lot of people have saved so much money with this simple letter. and I want you to be one more who take advantage of this great tool. if you do save some money with this. I want your feedback and comments will be beneficial to other readers. (please send your feedback to creditmatter@gmail.com

If you have collections in your report and are in debt. This will help you save money, in the next page you will find an example letter to negotiate your debt, this could save you up to thousands of dollars like it did for many people who used it. It's very simple all you have to do is re-type it fill out the information required. One other way it's to negotiate your creditors over the phone but you have to be good

at it. I have saved thousands of dollars for my clients on the phone. this is because when your account it's on collections you no longer owe to the primary creditor. this means that the creditor tried to collect their payment without success and sold your debt to a collections company sometimes for a fraction of the original amount. Therefore you can negotiate and save.

Sample Letter Requesting Reduced Payment

Date

Your Name
Address
City, State Zip

Creditor's Name
Address
City, State, Zip

Re: Account Number

Dear Creditor:
I am temporarily out of work because of
_____, and my income
has been severely reduced.
I am asking for your cooperation during this difficult
period.
Until I return to work, I need to cut back on all my
regular payments. I am proposing
to pay $_____ to you for a temporary period,
instead of the regular payment of
$_____.
When I return to work, I will work with you on a plan to
catch up on my payments.
Thank you for your understanding and consideration.
You may reach me at the number below.

Your Signature
Account Number
Address
City, State, Zip
Phone Number

Finally, a Painless Way to Buy a Car!

Purchasing a CarMax car is different from purchasing a car at a traditional dealership. Each CarMax dealership is designed so that the customer feels comfortable from the very beginning. The salespeople take turns greeting each new customer, so there is no competition for who will get there first. Since all of the employees are paid the same commission for each vehicle, there is no need for them to steer anyone toward a more expensive car. When a customer walks into the dealership, the salesperson will greet them and then allow them to shop in the manner that suits them best.

Digital Inventory

A unique feature of CarMax dealerships is their digital inventory kiosks. When a salesperson first greets a customer, he or she will guide that customer toward a kiosk that contains information about every vehicle in stock. Customers can use the kiosk computer to search for cars based on price, age, or model. The kiosk allows customers to compare different cars side by side without ever having to walk through the lot. When the customer narrows their selections down to a few vehicles, the salesperson can take them directly to those vehicles so that they can look at them more closely.

Reliable Pricing

The way that CarMax prices their vehicles is also a little different than you would find in a traditional dealership. Each car displays the full price prominently on the windshield. Salespeople do not have the power to change the stated price for any reason, so negotiation is not necessary. The stated price also includes any incidental fees that might have traditionally been assessed during the transaction. A customer can look at the price and know that there will be no changes between the stated cost and the final cost of the vehicle.

Vehicle History Reports

As part of the purchase process, each customer is provided with the opportunity to look at the AutoCheck vehicle history report of each vehicle. CarMax uses AutoCheck reports as a way to make sure that the cars they sell are in good condition and have not been rebuilt after serious accidents. The AutoCheck report also provides a detailed history of the car's maintenance, which provides information about any possible problems that occur often with the car. AutoCheck is an easy way for CarMax to ensure that each car on their lot meets their quality standards before they add the car to their inventory in the first place. It's also the easiest report to read of all available brands, meaning you can easily understand the history of the car you are considering with a simple numbered score.

Technology Is Changing the Way We Purchase Used Cars

There are significant advantages to purchasing used cars from dealers. For starters, you have the opportunity to get genuine feedback from a professional who matches people to vehicles every day. Even more, you have a company to fall back on if things turn out badly. As technology evolves, and the service industry changes, we might see different trends in this market, and the changes might be bigger than you think.

Buying a Car via an App

They're still gaining popularity, but there are some new mobile applications trying to match buyers with sellers using a peer-to-peer search tool for used cars. These apps essentially sell a premium listing service so effective that there is a 30-day "Will-Be-Sold" guarantee to sellers.

These apps also assure buyers by automatically requesting a certified mechanic to perform an 185-point inspection on the vehicles. This gives the seller an advantage in a demanding online market by providing crucial details that draw the attention of buyers, such as photos and accurate mileage readings. The vehicle will even be delivered to the buyer with only a small commission taken. These smart service-based strategies might be the key to a bright future for similar companies.

Virtual Reality and Dealerships

Several Virtual Reality headset manufacturers have already hit the market running, some with multi-billion dollar buyouts. But with the advent of these sorts of applications and technologies, is it that far-fetched to assume that many future dealerships might change their approach? Imagine vehicle simulations that allow test-driving of any of the millions of used cars on the market. Think about the possibility of customizing exactly what you want in a car: make, model, color, and engine, and then being shown a virtual model of your vehicle. The simulation could even account for damage or changes to the vehicle from wear and tear. The level of detail is astounding.

Finally, as we reflect on the impact this may have on dealerships, it's important to realize the necessity of human interaction in the buying and selling process. People are much more likely to make a decision with the encouragement, or pressure, of a salesperson involved. Will this mean future dealers come to you virtually and allow you to browse inventories of thousands of makes and models, all of which can be shipped to your location at the click of a button? That may, in fact, be the system we are reaching for.

For more visit these links at:

www.carvana.com,

www.fair.com

www.vroom.com,

www.truecar.com,

www.edmunds.com

www.kbb.com

www.carfax.com

This book is for information and education purposes only. Some of the examples and stories are used for illustration of the main idea to be transmitted to the reader. The amazing information is mainly from the several years of the author's experience in the car industry. The author nor his partners are financial advisers therefore they cannot give advise on the matter of investing or purchasing any assets. All information in this book is intended to save the consumer time and money. But it is solely the buyer's responsibility to do his/her due diligence when comes to investing their money on a vehicle. We are not liable for any wrong doing of the car dealerships nor in the amount of money you can save with this information. This will be only achieved by the hard work and good research of the buyer. All Rights Reserved. Mario Esteban

contact : 973-384-5592

Made in the USA
Middletown, DE
24 April 2019